MEDAL OF HONOR

Ryan Pitts

MEDAL OF HONOR

Ryan Pitts

Afghanistan: A Firefight
in the Mountains of Wanat

MICHAEL P. SPRADLIN

FARRAR STRAUS GIROUX
NEW YORK

Farrar Straus Giroux Books for Young Readers
An imprint of Macmillan Publishing Group, LLC
175 Fifth Avenue, New York, NY 10010

Text copyright © 2019 by Michael P. Spradlin
Map copyright © 2019 by Gene Thorpe, Cartographic Concepts, Inc.
All rights reserved
Printed in the United States of America
by LSC Communications, Crawfordsville, Indiana
Designed by Eileen Gilshian and Cassie Gonzales
First edition, 2019
Hardcover: 10 9 8 7 6 5 4 3 2 1
Paperback: 10 9 8 7 6 5 4 3 2 1

mackids.com

Library of Congress Control Number: 2018944888
ISBN 978-1-250-15711-9 (hardcover) / ISBN 978-1-250-15710-2 (paperback) /
ISBN 978-1-250-15709-6 (ebook)

Our books may be purchased in bulk for promotional, educational, or business
use. Please contact your local bookseller or the Macmillan Corporate and
Premium Sales Department at (800) 221-7945, ext. 5442, or by email at
MacmillanSpecialMarkets@macmillan.com.

The appearance of U.S. Department of Defense visual information
does not imply or constitute DOD endorsement.

This book is dedicated to all the men of Chosen Company, and in remembrance of the nine Sky Soldiers who made the ultimate sacrifice at the Battle of Wanat.

They hover as a cloud of witnesses over the nation.
—Henry Ward Beecher

CONTENTS

U.S. ARMY RANKS

Partial list, from lowest to highest

Private
Specialist
Corporal
Sergeant
Staff Sergeant
First Sergeant
Command Sergeant Major
Second Lieutenant
First Lieutenant
Captain
Major
Lieutenant Colonel
Colonel
Brigadier General
Major General
Lieutenant General
General

The ranks corporal through command sergeant major are noncommissioned officers. They are enlisted soldiers who rose through the ranks and don't have a commission. Commissioned officers—second lieutenants on up—generally have a college degree. They are often graduates of a military academy or a university's Reserve Officers' Training Corps program. In World War II, to replace officers lost in combat, enlisted men showing exceptional leadership were given battlefield commissions and promoted to second lieutenant. Commissioned officers who began their military careers as enlisted soldiers are referred to as Mustangs.

U.S. ARMY UNITS AND SIZES

Army Unit and Size	Number of Soldiers	Commanding Officer
Field Army = 2 or more Corps	50,000–250,000	Four-Star General
Corps = 2–5 Divisions	20,000–45,000	Three-Star Lieutenant General
Division = 3–4 Brigades	10,000–15,000	Two-Star Major General
Brigade/Regiment* = 3–5 Battalions	3,000–5,000	Colonel
Battalion/Regiment* = 4–6 Companies	200–1,000	Lieutenant Colonel
Company = 3–4 Platoons	50–200	Captain
Platoon = 3–4 Squads	15–40	Lieutenant
Squad = 10 Soldiers	10	Staff Sergeant

The number of soldiers in each unit varies depending on where it is deployed, its mission, and the available personnel, or individual unit strength.

* Before 1957, regiments were brigade-level units of about three thousand men, containing three battalions, artillery, and other supporting units, commanded by a colonel. Since then, the army has largely eliminated regiments as a command unit, with a few exceptions. Special Forces, Rangers, and armored cavalry still use brigade-level regiments, while today some army airborne units comprise battalion-level regiments commanded by a lieutenant colonel.

MEDAL OF HONOR

Ryan Pitts

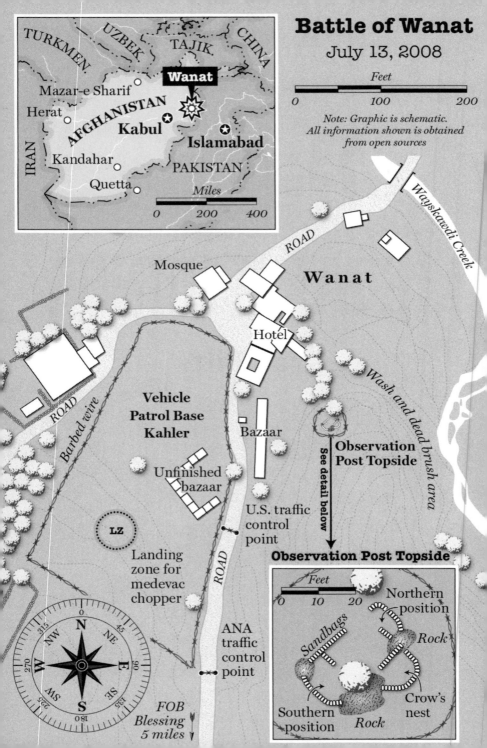

Battle of Wanat
July 13, 2008

Feet

0   100   200

*Note: Graphic is schematic.
All information shown is obtained
from open sources*

Inset map (Afghanistan/Pakistan region):
TURKMEN. UZBEK. TAJIK. CHINA
Mazar-e Sharif
Herat
IRAN
AFGHANISTAN
Kabul
Kandahar
Quetta
Wanat
Islamabad
PAKISTAN

Miles

0   200   400

Main map labels:

Wayskawedi Creek

ROAD

Mosque

Wanat

Hotel

Wash and dead brush area

Observation Post Topside

See detail below

Vehicle Patrol Base Kahler

Barbed wire

ROAD

Bazaar

Unfinished bazaar

U.S. traffic control point

LZ

Landing zone for medevac chopper

ROAD

ANA traffic control point

Compass rose: N, NE, E, SE, S, SW, W, NW (0, 45, 90, 135, 180, 225, 270, 315)

FOB Blessing 5 miles ↓

Observation Post Topside

Feet

0   10   20

Northern position

Sandbags

Rock

Crow's nest

Southern position

Rock

SURPRISE ATTACK

Wanat village
Nuristan Province, Afghanistan
July 13, 2008, 4:00 a.m.

WELL BEFORE SUNRISE, THE MEN OF SECOND PLATOON,
Chosen Company, were ordered to "stand to." Dressed
in full battle gear and ready to fight, the soldiers took up
their positions on the perimeter of Vehicle Patrol Base
Kahler. The paratroopers in the U.S. Army's famed
173rd Airborne Brigade had arrived in the village of
Wanat, in eastern Afghanistan, on July 8 to secure the
area and begin setting up the new outpost.

As a vehicle patrol base, Kahler was designed to
provide a launching pad for patrols in an area that
was known to be dangerous. Soldiers in high-mobility
multipurpose wheeled vehicles (popularly known as

Left to right: Sergeant Matthew Gobble, Sergeant Ryan Pitts, Sergeant Adam Delaney, Sergeant Dylan Meyer, Sergeant Brian Hissong, Sergeant Mike Santiago, and Sergeant Israel Garcia at FOB Blessing, summer 2007

Humvees) would provide security and look for signs of insurgents. The army planners hoped that the base's occupants would establish a connection with the local population and discourage enemy fighters from traveling through the area.

Upon arriving, the men of Chosen Company had commenced building up the VPB's defenses. Once they had secured the area with basic obstacles such as concertina wire, sandbags, and antivehicle ditches, army engineers would construct the rest of the installation. To the east of the base, on a small, terraced hill, Second Platoon established an observation post called OP Topside to provide clear views of the valley.

If VPB Kahler was a sailing vessel, then OP Topside was the crow's nest, sitting above the small command post in the center of the base. Topside was protected by sandbags about waist-high—sandbags that had been filled by the soldiers a spadeful at a time in the sweltering heat. Inside Topside were a long-range surveillance system, machine guns, and a grenade launcher, as well as ammunition, grenades, and other supplies. The store of water was limited and was being rationed carefully.

The observation post butted up against a steep ravine that was overgrown with vegetation. It was a

Members of Chosen Company unpack gear before digging in at Wanat

View from the Northeast of Wanat village, with mosque and hotel in foreground. Vehicles at center indicate position of VPB Kahler; tree at far left in front of terraced fields marks position of OP Topside.

vulnerability, and the platoon had strung coils of concertina wire all along the edge to discourage an attack from that direction. Every night, the paratroopers placed antipersonnel mines inside the wire for extra security, recovering them at first light.

As the American soldiers established their base, "it definitely felt like we were being watched," recalled Sergeant Ryan Pitts. "There were a lot of men sitting along the rock walls outside of the perimeter by the bazaar, or by the hotel; sitting and having tea, just spending a lot of time watching what we were doing."

Up at OP Topside in the predawn darkness of July 13, Sergeant Ryan Pitts took his position with eight other paratroopers: Sergeant Matthew Gobble and Specialists Jonathan Ayers, Jason Bogar, Matthew Phillips, Pruitt Rainey, Tyler Stafford, and Gunnar Zwilling, along with Private Chris McKaig. The platoon leader, Lieutenant Jonathan Brostrom, and the current platoon sergeant, David Dzwik, had given Pitts command of the observation post. Brostrom and Dzwik remained in the command center down the hill at VPB Kahler. If any action was needed, Brostrom would coordinate from there.

It was quiet in the village, but all the soldiers had a

07/12/2008

Northern crow's nest position inside OP Topside, one day before the battle

Paratroopers of the 503rd Regiment landing on Corregidor Island, February 16, 1945

NAMES OF HONOR

OP Topside took its name from an important event in the history of Chosen Company's 503rd Regiment—the 1945 attack on Corregidor Island, at the entrance of Manila Bay in the Philippines, a famous American victory against the Japanese during World War II. The steep, high ground on the western part of the island was called Topside. In a surprise attack from the air, paratroopers from the 503rd landed on Topside, jumping from an altitude of only four hundred feet onto the rocky terrain. An amphibious assault force landed on beaches to the east, and after two weeks of brutal fighting, U.S. forces had control of the island.

Chosen Company's Second Platoon named Vehicle Patrol Base Kahler after Platoon Sergeant Matthew R. Kahler, who had been killed in action six months earlier.

sense that something was up. It felt "a little bit odd," Pitts said later, which he thought was possibly an "indication of what might be coming. Every day leading up to July thirteenth, at the crack of dawn, people were out there working the fields, and that morning, no one was out there. Oftentimes, in some of the other fights I've been in, in Afghanistan, the locals sometimes know that it's coming, and you can get a sense that something might happen because no one's around. It's kind of a ghost town."

As a forward observer for his platoon, it was Pitts's job to prepare targets and coordinates for artillery directed at any insurgents in the area. If he or his team spotted an enemy location, he was to report back to the company commander, Captain Matthew Myer, at VPB Kahler. Pitts had set up targets for mortar and artillery fire based on his experience in previous fights and where he believed an attack was likely to come from. If required, he could call in mortars, artillery fire, or support from aircraft.

105-mm howitzer and M252 mortar

THE BIG GUNS

Artillery is any large, heavy weapon designed to shoot munitions across long distances, from the catapults of antiquity, to sixteenth-century cannons, to modern-day howitzers. Today's artillery pieces can fire projectiles from dozens of miles away with great precision. Chosen Company had three pieces of artillery in place at Wanat, two mortars and an antitank missile launcher mounted on a Humvee. Two 155-mm howitzers five miles away at Forward Operating Base Blessing would also provide fire for VPB Kahler whenever necessary.

Mortars are a smaller, specialized type of artillery. Their lighter, shorter tubes are designed to quickly launch shells at a higher arc and shorter distance than regular artillery. VPB Kahler had a 60-mm mortar, which could fire up to thirty rounds a minute, and a heavier, longer-range 120-mm, which could fire up to sixteen rounds a minute.

It was not long after taking their positions that soldiers manning the missile truck down at the base spotted potential insurgents moving in the hills to the west in the predawn light. At OP Topside Sergeant Pitts trained the surveillance system on them and started to put together coordinates for mortar fire. Before he could radio the mortar pit, however, a burst of machine-gun fire came from the north, at 4:20 a.m.

It was the signal for an attack to begin.

The area erupted in a hail of bullets and rocket-propelled grenades from all directions. "The whole valley lit up," Pitts later said.

In the opening salvo, shrapnel from a grenade hit the mortar pit at VPB Kahler, severely injuring Private Sergio S. Abad. The mortarman nonetheless continued to hand rifle ammunition to his sergeant until the order came to evacuate the pit. Only after soldiers pulled Abad to the cover of the command post did they discover that his wounds were critical. Abad died in the midst of the battle.

As many as two hundred enemy fighters were attacking. The forty-nine Americans at VPB Kahler were seriously outnumbered.

The Battle of Wanat was underway.

AFGHANISTAN AND THE WAR ON TERROR

ON SEPTEMBER 11, 2001, THE UNITED STATES EXPERIENCED the worst terrorist attack in its history. Extremists hijacked four flights originating from three U.S. airports. After taking control of the planes, the terrorists crashed two into the twin towers of the World Trade Center in New York City, killing and injuring thousands of people. A third plane was crashed into the Pentagon in Washington, D.C., causing the deaths and injuries of hundreds more. The fourth did not reach its target. Passengers on that flight fought back against the hijackers, causing the aircraft to crash in a field in rural Pennsylvania, killing everybody on board.

The moment the south tower of the World Trade Center was hit, September 11, 2001. Ninety minutes later, both towers had collapsed.

The United States found evidence implicating the terrorist group Al Queda in the attack. Al Queda (Arabic for "the base") is a militant network created by Osama bin Laden, a wealthy Saudi Arabian who had fought with Afghan rebels against the Soviet Union in the 1980s. Bin Laden considered the United States another threat to Islam, and he trained Islamic militants in Sudan to fight U.S. interests around the world. After Sudan expelled him in 1996, Bin Laden returned to Afghanistan, where he found sympathy in the Taliban, an ultra-conservative religious and political faction that was taking control of the country.

Afghanistan, a mountainous country in central Asia, is bordered to the north by former Soviet states, to the south and east by Pakistan, and to the west by Iran. It has a turbulent history dating back to ancient times, as the repeated target of attempted conquest and occupation. Alexander the Great is said to have remarked after he invaded the area in 329 B.C., Afghanistan "is easy to march into but hard to march out of."

Since the 1980s, Afghanistan has been torn apart by war and strife. In 1979 the Soviet Union invaded the country to prop up a communist government opposed by the country's devoutly Muslim and largely anticommunist population. For ten years Afghan rebels fought the Soviets and the communist government before the Soviet Union finally pulled out in 1989, after having lost over fifteen thousand soldiers.

When the Soviets left, Afghanistan descended into chaos. Warlords and militia groups controlled various areas. With all the fighting, the capital city of Kabul was reduced to rubble. Claiming he had a vision to restore order, Mullah Mohammad Omar led a group of religious students, the Taliban, to take over the southeastern city of Kandahar.

Soon the Taliban subdued the warlords in the southern part of the country. With help from conservative

Taliban fighters in Afghanistan

AMERICA'S WAR ON TERROR

Nine days after the terrorist attack on America, President George W. Bush declared war on terror in a speech delivered to a joint session of Congress. The war would become known as Operation Enduring Freedom:

On September the 11th, enemies of freedom committed an act of war against our country . . .

Americans are asking: Who attacked our country? The evidence we have gathered all points to a collection of loosely affiliated terrorist organizations known as Al Queda . . .

The terrorists practice a fringe form of Islamic extremism that has been rejected by Muslim scholars and the vast majority of Muslim clerics—a fringe movement that perverts the peaceful teachings of Islam . . .

The leadership of Al Queda has great influence in Afghanistan and supports the Taliban regime in controlling most of that country. In Afghanistan, we see Al Queda's vision for the world . . .

The United States respects the people of Afghanistan—after all, we are currently its largest source of humanitarian aid—but we condemn the Taliban regime. It is not only repressing its own people, it is threatening people everywhere . . .

The enemy of America is not our many Muslim friends; it is not our many Arab friends. Our enemy is a radical network of terrorists, and every government that supports them.

Our war on terror begins with Al Queda, but it . . . will not end until every terrorist group of global reach has been found, stopped, and defeated. Americans are asking, why do they hate us? . . . They hate our freedoms—our freedom of religion, our freedom of speech, our freedom to vote and assemble and disagree with each other . . .

With every atrocity, they hope that America grows fearful, retreating from the world and forsaking our friends . . .

By sacrificing human life to serve their radical visions—by abandoning every value except the will to power—they follow in the path of fascism, and Nazism, and totalitarianism. And they will follow that path all the way, to where it ends: in history's unmarked grave of discarded lies.

Islamic elements outside the country, the militant group took over city after city. By 1996 Kabul had fallen, and the Taliban controlled its government. It supported Al Queda and gave the terrorist organization a relatively safe base to operate from.

World leaders from many countries tried several times to arrange a cease-fire between the Taliban and its remaining foes in northern Afghanistan. But the agreements never lasted long, and by 2001 the Taliban had control of 90 percent of the country.

The Taliban enacted strict laws prohibiting everything from chess sets to CDs and any form of Western entertainment, claiming these things violated Muslim law. Non-Muslim women were required to wear veils and cover themselves. Minorities in the country were required to wear identification tags. The Taliban imposed harsh penalties on anyone who broke the rules.

A month after the events of September 11, 2001, the United States led coalition forces into Afghanistan to seek out Bin Laden and destroy Al Queda. They worked with anti-Taliban allies in the country and, two months of hard fighting later, the Taliban was toppled and a new central government was created. Without a safe haven, Bin Laden and Al Queda were forced into the mountainous border region of neighboring Pakistan, but Afghanistan's problems did not go away. The Taliban regrouped. It was easy for insurgents to come out of hiding, carry out an attack, and slip away, blending seamlessly with the civilians. Suicide bombings against local citizens and the military alike increased. Rival militias reemerged to provide security in rural areas where the Afghan government and U.S. forces couldn't.

FBI wanted poster for the fugitive Al Queda leader Osama bin Laden, who was killed by U.S. Special Forces during an early-morning raid in Pakistan in May 2011

The war continues today, even after Bin Laden's death in 2011. Outside extremist groups who see the West as a threat to Islam in general have joined the Taliban's fight in Afghanistan. The U.S. military and its allies fight on.

Afghanistan's tortured history set the stage for the Battle of Wanat, which would become another chapter in that history.

DIRECT HIT

AUTOMATIC-WEAPONS FIRE AND ROCKET-PROPELLED
grenades rained down on OP Topside. All nine paratroopers in the observation post were hit in the initial
attack. Sergeant Pitts was struck by shrapnel in both
legs and his left arm. Hurled through the air, he landed
in a heap, the wind knocked out of him. A piece of shrapnel had penetrated his right thigh. When he could
gather his thoughts, he worried it might have pierced a
major blood vessel. Unable to apply his own tourniquet,
he needed another pair of hands.

"I'd been a little shell-shocked . . . I had taken

shrapnel to both my legs and . . . couldn't move my feet, couldn't use my legs, just from shock."

Not able to stand, Pitts crawled to the southern end of the observation post, where he heard his team returning fire. There he found Sergeant Gobble wounded and shell-shocked. Specialist Jason Bogar was firing his machine gun, but stopped long enough to apply a tourniquet to Pitts's leg. Specialist Tyler Stafford, badly wounded himself, crawled over.

"Sergeant! We lost Zwilling and Phillips," he shouted over the noise.

Specialist Gunnar Zwilling had been killed in the opening barrage. Specialist Matthew Phillips had managed to return fire and throw a hand grenade before he, too, was killed. Stafford said he thought the enemy was throwing grenades as well as using rocket launchers.

The observation post was surrounded and taking heavy fire. Still unable to stand, Pitts crawled to the northern position of the post, where the team had stored extra ammo and grenades. The enemy had infiltrated the brush-filled ravine just a few meters away,

"My line of thinking was, if they can throw hand grenades, so can we," Pitts said later.

Pitts grabbed the grenades and, one by one, "cooked

Specialist Tyler Stafford (front left), Corporal Matthew B. Phillips (front right), and Specialist Gunnar Zwilling, spring 2008

"COOKING OFF" A GRENADE

This risky maneuver means pulling the pin and releasing the safety lever to trigger the fuse, then holding the grenade for a few seconds before throwing it. This allows the fuse to burn down so the grenade detonates before it strikes the ground or immediately after, preventing an enemy from picking it up and throwing it back before it explodes. It is a dangerous tactic. There is a one in five chance the grenade might have a short fuse and explode before it can be thrown.

M67 fragmentation grenades

them off" for a few seconds before throwing them into the brush. This brave move bought some time as the insurgents were temporarily driven back by the explosions.

Despite his injuries, shock, and blood loss, Pitts radioed a situation report to Captain Myer, the company commander, down at the patrol base. He requested urgent help, and in between lobbing grenades, he reported on casualties and estimated the enemy positions. Trying to conserve grenades, Sergeant Pitts crawled over to a M240 machine gun. Sitting up, he blindly pulled the trigger to fire over the wall of sandbags. Eventually he managed to prop himself up on his knees and lay down suppressing fire. Without an assistant gunner to handle the ammunition, though, the gun repeatedly jammed. Pitts would pull the twenty-seven-pound gun down, clear it, and fire blindly again until he could prop himself back up.

While Pitts and the remaining paratroopers in OP Topside were fighting for their lives, VPB Kahler was also taking heavy, sustained fire. The insurgents had

A U.S. marine fires an M240 machine gun.

focused their initial volleys on the major weapons systems. The missile truck exploded, scattering missiles and flames everywhere. One of the two truck-mounted .50-caliber machine guns was also taken out. From the mortar pit, soldiers managed to shoot four rounds of high explosives at the insurgents on the western hills using Pitts's coordinates before a rocket hit the stack of ammunition, forcing the men to evacuate.

In the command center, Captain Myer notified FOB Blessing of the attack and requested immediate support from artillery, aircraft, and the quick-reaction force stationed at the base, a ninety-minute drive away. Within minutes, Blessing's 155-mm howitzers opened fire on Pitts's prearranged targets. But the enemy was too close to U.S. soldiers for the big guns to be used safely, limiting their effectiveness. Myer faced a similar issue with the platoon's two truck-mounted grenade launchers. The enemy positions were so close that the grenades would simply overshoot them.

Despite the heavy damage already inflicted on VPB Kahler, Captain Myer knew things would get worse if the insurgents managed to capture OP Topside. From there they would be able to fire directly down into the base. But he was running out of weapons and ammunition to allocate. Somehow, they needed to hold on until support arrived.

It was intense and chaotic, but the Topside paratroopers fought on, unwilling to let the insurgents overrun their position. If they received air support or reinforcements, they thought they could turn back the attackers.

Pitts and his team didn't know it yet, but help was on the way.

The question was, would it get there in time?

LEARNING ON THE JOB

RYAN PITTS WAS BORN IN LOWELL, MASSACHUSETTS, but spent most of his early years in southern New Hampshire.

"My graduating class was about a hundred and fifty, two hundred, so really small. I liked being outdoors, playing paintball, little bit of hunting, riding four-wheelers, things like that, getting into trouble with my friends."

As for joining the military, Pitts said, "I had grown up always wanting to serve. I had a tremendous amount of respect for service members." But it wasn't until 2003, during his senior year of high school, that he decided to enlist. "I had been accepted to college but didn't know what I wanted to do."

At age seventeen, Pitts joined the army under the delayed-enlistment program. Soon after high school he was on his way to Fort Sill in Lawton, Oklahoma, for ten weeks of basic combat training and another eight weeks of training at the U.S. Army Field Artillery School to become a forward observer.

"My job was to control indirect-fire assets, such as mortars and artillery, close-combat aviation such as Apaches, and close air support such as F-15s, AC-130s, any sort of attack aircraft."

Pitts volunteered for airborne school and moved on to Fort Benning, Georgia, to train as a paratrooper. After

he received his airborne badge, he joined the 173rd Airborne Brigade at Camp Ederle, Italy. Pitts arrived in February 2004, just as the 173rd was returning from combat in Iraq. He remembers being intimidated as the "new guy" in the brigade.

173rd Airborne Brigade shoulder badge

THE FORWARD OBSERVER: A GUNNER'S EYES

Indirect-fire assets are weapons that are aimed by coordinates or other measurements. Whoever operates the weapons relies on precise calculations provided by the forward observer. This is opposed to direct fire, where gunners have a line of sight to the target.

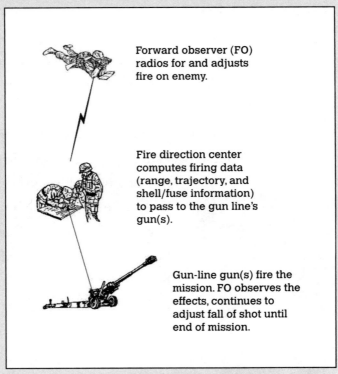

Forward observer (FO) radios for and adjusts fire on enemy.

Fire direction center computes firing data (range, trajectory, and shell/fuse information) to pass to the gun line's gun(s).

Gun-line gun(s) fire the mission. FO observes the effects, continues to adjust fall of shot until end of mission.

Schematic of the forward observer in action

"All these guys had been at war for a year, and I'm the new guy, and I always say, I had seen enough movies to know you don't want to be the new guy."

The veterans were rough on the new guys. "You had to prove yourself," Pitts recalled. "But there was a point to it, kind of this toughening up. If you can't handle that, then you can't handle what the real job is."

In April 2005, Pitts made his first deployment to Afghanistan for the latest phase in Operation Enduring Freedom.

The 173rd worked in southeastern Afghanistan, mainly in the provinces of Zabol, Helmand, and Kandahar. Chosen Company was part of a battalion of five hundred soldiers responsible for the security of an area roughly the size of Massachusetts, Connecticut, and Rhode Island combined.

On May 3, Pitts was involved in his first major firefight.

"That was kind of my first baptism by fire. I actually didn't end up doing my job. One of the infantry guys went down. We weren't using artillery, so I jumped into the infantry slot. But that was kind of the nature of that deployment. I didn't control too many indirect-fire assets, mortars from time to time. I spent more time

controlling close air support and combat aviation—
which are important, incredibly important, assets—
and also learning the jobs of others around me."

During that first deployment, Pitts's infantry platoon
fought in a lot of missions using Humvees and had "a
number of air assault missions, flying in, in helicopters,
to press the fight to the enemy."

The new members of the 173rd were gaining valuable
skills during this deployment—experience that would
prove invaluable during the Battle of Wanat. Training is
important, but it is no substitute for actual combat.

In spring 2006, the deployment ended, and the 173rd
Airborne Brigade returned to Italy. After a year in
Afghanistan, the soldiers had tremendous confidence in
their ability as a fighting force.

Pitts took thirty days of leave. "That was about the
only time I made it home. The rest of my time was spent
in Italy training up for that next deployment."

For twelve months, members of the 173rd rested up,
trained, and prepared. The rumor was that they would
be shipped to Iraq, but they later learned they would be
returning to Afghanistan. This time they were headed to
a more rugged and mountainous area in the country's

OPERATION ENDURING FREEDOM

On October 7, 2001, air strikes began in the skies over Afghanistan. Operation Enduring Freedom was underway. It was an all-out assault on the Taliban, which had given Al Queda and other terrorist groups a safe haven. A coalition of nations joined the United States, including Canada, Great Britain, Germany, France, and Turkey. They worked with Afghan militias that had been fighting the Taliban for years.

In November, the Afghan militias took the capital city of Kabul without a fight. In December the Taliban lost its last stronghold in the city of Kandahar. With the Taliban routed, Hamid Karzai, a tribal leader from southern Afghanistan, was selected as the country's interim leader. After a new constitution was approved in 2004, Karzai became the country's first elected president.

In December 2014, President Obama declared Operation Enduring Freedom over. Since then, U.S. military forces remaining in Afghanistan function under Operation Freedom's Sentinel.

northeast. The deployment would begin in 2007 and span fifteen months.

The northeastern provinces of Kunar and Nuristan

share a long, unguarded border with Pakistan. This part of Afghanistan was not primarily Taliban territory, but the villagers were resistant to the American presence and the Afghan central government. The area also attracted foreign fighters from outside extremist groups who could easily cross back and forth over the Pakistani border to engage U.S. and coalition forces.

On July 8, 2008, with three weeks left in its deployment, Chosen Company's Second Platoon arrived in the village of Wanat. Along with the platoon were two dozen soldiers of the Afghan National Army and three U.S. marines embedded with them to observe and train.

A U.S. soldier approaches a village in the mountainous Kunar Province

In a few short days, they would all discover just how resistant the area was to an American presence. Wanat would become one of the United States' deadliest battles in the war.

And Ryan Pitts would find himself right in the middle of it.

A U.S. soldier with an M4 rifle mounted with an M203 grenade launcher—the weapon that Ryan Pitts used to fend off nearby enemy attackers at OP Topside

ALL ALONE

THE PARATROOPERS AT OP TOPSIDE CONTINUED TO KEEP the enemy at bay with a constant barrage of fire. Specialist Bogar kept "loading and spraying" with his light machine gun in the southern position. Above him in the crow's nest, gunners Ayers, McKaig, and Rainey were furiously running the heavier M240. They didn't have time to think about help or reinforcements. They were fighting for their lives.

Knowing that maintaining control of OP Topside was paramount, platoon leader Lieutenant Jonathan Brostrom and Specialist Jason Hovater made their way to the

A view of the casualty collection point at OP Topside the day after the battle

observation post from VPB Kahler's perimeter. Enemy fighters had stored weapons in the hotel overlooking the base before the attack and were firing incessantly from their high perch. To the men of Chosen Company, it felt as if their attackers would never run out of ammunition. Brostrom and Hovater ran headlong through this hailstorm of fire. As they sprinted across the open space between the hotel and the bazaar and scrambled up the terraces, bullets riddled the ground at their feet.

Their arrival at Topside caught Sergeant Pitts completely by surprise.

"Later on—I don't know how much time had passed since I had thrown hand grenades and gotten on the machine gun—Lt. Brostrom arrived at the OP, and he popped his head up over the sandbags to the west, right at the edge of that northern position. It startled me because I wasn't expecting him. He and Spc. Hovater had left Vehicle Patrol Base Kahler and made a run to reinforce the OP. They had cut through the bazaar/hotel area [and] exposed themselves to direct enemy fire. There was no cover. I honestly don't know how they made it. They probably shouldn't have made it. They may have just surprised the enemy [by taking that] route, and so they came to reinforce the OP."

Pitts informed Lieutenant Brostrom of the conditions at OP Topside and the suspected enemy locations. Specialist Pruitt Rainey, who had been managing weapons and ammunition during the firefight, exchanged an M203 grenade launcher for Pitts's machine gun and went with Brostrom and Hovater to establish a defensive position in Topside's sleeping area. Pitts was the last one to see any of them alive. Insurgents inside the wire perimeter killed the three paratroopers as they were setting up their position.

In the crow's nest, Ayers and McKaig fired furious bursts from their M240 machine gun until they ran out of ammunition. Then they continued the fight with two M4 rifles. McKaig later remembered, "Me and Ayers also had a fire from an explosion that caught some of our equipment on fire. I remember engaging the enemy and trying to kick out the fire at the same time. I remember telling myself 'The Army never trained me for this kind of situation.'"

Ayers and McKaig's technique at this point was to pop up together at intervals above the sandbags, fire off six to nine rounds at whatever muzzle flashes they could detect, then drop back down. They continued to expose themselves even after Ayers took a hit in the helmet. Eventually Ayers was hit with an armor-piercing bullet and killed. After firing twelve magazines, McKaig's weapon became too hot to reload. He reached for Ayers's weapon, only to discover it had been rendered useless by the AK-47 rounds that killed his comrade.

Specialist Bogar, meanwhile, tried to suppress the enemy fire coming from the hotel and the bazaar. Known in the platoon to be utterly fearless, Bogar jumped up and left the observation post, trying to get closer to his targets. He was later found killed by enemy fire outside the perimeter of Topside.

With no weapons, McKaig left the crow's nest and joined Sergeant Gobble and Specialist Stafford, who lay wounded at the southern end of the observation post. To his surprise, he found a rocket launcher in a nearby tree. He managed to set it off, stopping the enemy fire for a few seconds. They needed more ammo, and McKaig was sent down to get it. Stafford was losing a lot of blood and had to be evacuated. Gobble called out to Pitts, but, receiving no answer, believed Pitts had died of his wounds, and they made their way down the terraces after McKaig.

What they didn't realize was that Pitts was still alive, maintaining radio contact with Captain Myer down in VPB Kahler, giving him updates and working up fire missions.

Pitts was not sure how much time passed before he realized he wasn't hearing return fire from inside OP Topside. If he called out to his comrades, he risked giving away his position to the enemy. Still losing blood from his wounds, he silently crawled around the observation post to assess the situation. To his dismay, he discovered that he was alone.

The enemy was no more than a few meters away. Pitts called Captain Myer on the radio, whispering so as not to reveal his position. "[I] got on the radio and told them everyone was either dead or gone except for me and if they didn't send anyone up here, the position was going to fall. I let them know that the enemy was really close."

For some reason, the insurgents had not yet rushed the observation post, perhaps uncertain of how many paratroopers remained, or suspicious of a counterattack. They were close, though. So close that those listening to Pitts on the radio could hear enemy voices around him.

But Captain Myer was in a desperate situation. He had no reinforcements to send.

Pitts was on his own.

"I thought it was my time. My biggest concern was [that] I didn't want to be taken alive."

Reeling from his wounds and the loss of his brothers, Pitts realized he might be able to buy a little more time. He remembered Sergeant Sean Samaroo showing his squad how to fire indirectly with a grenade launcher, to drop rounds where they couldn't see. The M203 had a range of about four hundred meters. But Sergeant Samaroo had instructed the squad to practice shooting the grenade launcher nearly straight up, angled slightly toward the enemy. This would fire the grenades in a very high arc so that they landed just twenty to thirty meters away—far enough that the shooter would remain outside the grenade's blast radius, but with deadly efficiency for any enemy that was closing in.

Pitts launched a grenade and watched it climb into the sky. At first he thought it was going to come straight back down on top of him. But it landed near the enemy.

Pitts heard the screams of injured insurgents. He fired again. "I was putting them right where I put the [hand] grenades and hoped the arc would bring them down into the riverbed."

He was certain air support was on the way. If he could hold on until it arrived, he thought he just might get out of this. He called on the radio for someone with a sightline to Topside to lay down fire over the tops of the sandbags. This would discourage any insurgents from attempting to storm the walls.

Sergeant Brian Hissong responded. From his position at the traffic-control point across the road from VPB Kahler, Hissong began laying down suppressing fire directly over Topside. Bullets flew inches above Pitts's head as he continued to fire grenades. Pitts recalled later that he had such confidence in his platoon mate's skill that he didn't even flinch at the proximity of the rounds. Bullets were flying over the sandbags and into the wash just beyond OP Topside, where the enemy crouched, waiting for a chance to attack. The fire kept the insurgents at bay and bought Pitts more time as he waited, hoping reinforcements would arrive.

His odds of survival were getting worse. But he refused to give up.

THE LEGACY OF THE 173RD AIRBORNE

THERE WAS A REASON RYAN PITTS AND HIS PLATOON mates were proud to join the Sky Soldiers of the 173rd Airborne Brigade Combat Team after airborne school. The unit has a long and storied history of being at the tip of the spear of American warfare since its formation in 1917.

It was first organized in World War I as the 173rd Infantry Brigade. In World War II, the 173rd was re-designated as the 87th Reconnaissance Troop and saw action as part of the famed "Stalwart and Strong" 87th Infantry Division, the Golden Acorn Division that fought in the Battle of the Bulge. Although not part of the brigade in World War II, the actions of the 503rd Parachute Infantry Regiment form an important part of the 173rd's lineage. That team earned its Rock Regiment nickname by jumping onto Corregidor Island in the Philippines in 1945 (see sidebar, p. 8).

In 1963, the 173rd was reactivated as the 173rd Airborne Brigade, incorporating the 503rd Regiment. As the U.S. paratroopers trained in the Pacific, their Nationalist Chinese allies called them *tien bien*, "sky soldiers." The Sky Soldiers arrived in Vietnam two years later.

Vietnam marked an important chapter in the unit's history. In more than six years of continuous combat, the Sky Soldiers of the 173rd were awarded 13 Medals of Honor, 46 Distinguished Service Crosses, 1,736 Silver Stars, and over 6,000 Purple Hearts. At Dak To in particular the Sky Soldiers became part of army lore.

Dak To is in Vietnam's

Unit badge of the 173rd Airborne Brigade, the Sky Soldiers

Central Highlands, close to the borders of Cambodia and Laos. Dense rain forest covers the mountains, and the valleys are choked with thick bamboo. In November 1967, the Battle of Dak To took a heavy toll on the brigade. The 173rd fought in difficult terrain with limited visibility against a well-trained, well-equipped, entrenched, and determined North Vietnamese enemy. The fighting was intense and at close quarters, some of it hand-to-hand.

On November 3, 1967, the 173rd arrived at its position at Hill 1338, south of Dak To. The next morning, when Alpha Company began moving up the hill, it was ambushed by a unit of the People's Army of Vietnam, the army of the North Vietnamese. The fighting was fierce. With Alpha Company desperate for reinforcements, Charlie Company was sent to assist—but the thick vegetation and rugged terrain made it difficult for them to move into a position to provide aid. Nor were they able to call in close air support. The jungle cover made it difficult for pilots to determine their targets.

But this was the 173rd—the Sky Soldiers. They carried the legacy of the men who jumped onto Corregidor in World War II. If necessary, they would fight to the last man.

U.S. troops at the battle of Dak To, 1967

Alpha Company dug in and put up a ferocious defense against the North Vietnamese. However, the enemy had trenches, bunkers, and tunnels on the high ground. Alpha Company held out, but at great cost. The North Vietnamese forces were experienced jungle fighters. They would attack in waves, then slip into the jungle like ghosts, only to reappear minutes or hours later.

The fighting went on for weeks as the 173rd tried to clear the area of North Vietnamese fighters. Once the 173rd was able to determine their locations, heavy artillery and mortars pounded the enemy positions. On November 19, the 173rd launched an assault against a last pocket of North Vietnamese dug in atop a hill to the southeast. The Charlie Company commander called it Hill 875, and it would see some of the most terrible fighting of the battle. Taking heavy casualties, the 173rd reached the first line of enemy bunkers on November 21, but night was falling. The Sky Soldiers would have to wait.

And wait some more, as the commander put off the final attack and called in more bomb runs. U.S. artillery and close air support bombarded the hilltop so savagely that it eliminated all the vegetation and ground cover. On November 23, the 173rd moved in only to find the enemy had once again slipped into the jungle, withdrawing across the borders into Laos and Cambodia.

For its actions at Dak To, the 173rd was awarded the Presidential Unit Citation for "extraordinary heroism in action against an armed enemy."

REINFORCEMENTS
7

Wanat village
Nuristan Province, Afghanistan
July 13, 2008, approximately 5:00 a.m.

RYAN PITTS WAS STILL ALONE IN OP TOPSIDE.

The command center at the patrol base was taking almost continuous fire from the insurgents. With radios damaged and soldiers wounded, communication was spotty at best. The company commander, Captain Matthew Myer, was desperate for air support to arrive.

Someone needed to reinforce OP Topside before the insurgents broke through. The enemy was practically on top of Sergeant Pitts. "Sergeant said in a hushed tone that he was hit, laying down behind cover, and could hear [insurgents] walking within ten meters (33 feet) of his position," recalled Sergeant Jonathan Benton, who was down at the command post.

At the traffic-control point across the road from the main base, Sergeant Sean Samaroo noticed the lack of fire coming from OP Topside. He decided on his own to send up reinforcements. He and two others had barely started up the hill when they ran into McKaig, Stafford, and Gobble coming down. Samaroo and his guys promptly brought the three evacuees back to the shelter of the traffic-control point to treat their injuries.

In the meantime, Sergeant Israel Garcia and Private Jacob Sones had sprinted over from the main base after hearing Pitts's desperate words to Captain Myer over the radio. They joined Samaroo and Specialist Michael Denton as reinforcements and set out for Topside with fresh ammunition.

Before crossing the open terraces, Sergeant Samaroo scanned the hillside, looking for enemy activity. He spied an insurgent firing into OP Topside from behind a boulder inside the post perimeter. Samaroo shot at the man, driving him back. The four paratroopers rushed up the hill, pouring extensive fire on the enemy positions. Their ferocious onslaught pushed the enemy out of

Ryan Pitts with Sergeant Israel Garcia, summer 2007

Topside, and the observation post was secured in American hands, if still only tenuously.

Sergeant Samaroo immediately set about strengthening the defenses. Denton put the M240 machine gun in the crow's nest back in action. Private Sones started to treat Pitts's wounds, and Sergeant Garcia pulled security in the center, keeping a lookout. "I definitely felt relief when Garcia, Samaroo, Sones, and Denton showed up," Pitts recalled. "It was, 'Thank God I'm not alone.' I was just glad that they were there. I didn't even care that they were trying to treat me. It was just good to know that they were there."

Just after Samaroo and his reinforcements arrived, insurgent forces launched another furious attack. Small-arms fire and rocket-propelled grenades poured into OP Topside. Apparently, the earlier lull in the fighting had allowed the enemy time to regroup. Specialist Denton recalled, "That's when my position was hit by, I believe, two RPGs, with a third hitting inside the actual OP . . . The blast blew me outside of my bunker, causing me to land on my head and neck, then the rest of my body hit the ground. I lost my weapon in the process. After that I started crawling to get away from the position by a few feet and I could hear everyone screaming, including my squad leader [Sergeant Samaroo], that he had been hit."

Despite his wounds and loss of blood, Sergeant Pitts clearly recalled the moment when the renewed attack began. "Sones was treating me against the north wall. I was sitting down and he was bandaging me up. That's when another volley of RPGs and hand grenades came in. I was hit again, as was Sones. That's when Garcia took a direct hit from an RPG. I thought he was dead from his wounds. I knew Samaroo and Denton were hit and I could hear Samaroo screaming that he was hit."

As OP Topside continued to receive heavy fire, Pitts crawled over to Sergeant Garcia, who was mortally wounded and rapidly fading. Pitts held his hand and comforted his brother-in-arms until he slipped away.

The situation was growing worse by the minute. Everyone was wounded, though they all still went about their duties. They gathered in the shelter of the post's southern fighting position and dragged Garcia's body in.

"Denton started pulling security to the east, despite being hurt, and Samaroo was doing the same to the north and west. Sones was pretty shell-shocked and Denton's hand was pretty messed up," Pitts said.

Denton recalled, "I couldn't fire with my right hand, it was hard to stand because both my legs had been hit, but I could stand and pull security to the east, where we were still receiving fire from the most, where they had snuck up on us and tried to overrun us."

The four men at OP Topside were prepared to do whatever was necessary to hold the line. But they desperately needed help.

Luckily, the cavalry was on the way.

CLOSE AIR SUPPORT

SINCE WORLD WAR II, AIRCRAFT AND INFANTRY HAVE
had an important relationship. The United States
entered that conflict believing that bombers would be
the principal weapon in the war against Nazi Germany
and the empire of Japan.

During World War II, the Army Air Forces—as the U.S.
Air Force was called then—used fighter aircraft like the
P-51 Mustang and the P-47 Thunderbolt to provide cover,
reconnaissance, and fire support to ground troops. They
were particularly effective against enemy tanks and
other armored vehicles. The Mustang, considered one

P-51 Mustang

of the greatest fighter planes ever made, was also useful
as a long-range escort for bombers.

When helicopters first came on the scene during the
war, the U.S. military used them for combat rescue in
Burma and the Pacific. The Germans had a handful for
reconnaissance. In the Korean War the Sioux helicopter,
the first in a long line of rotary aircraft named after Native
American nations, was used primarily for medical evacuation. As engines became bigger and stronger, helicopters began to haul cargo and personnel and participate
in air assaults.

Although not as fast as a jet fighter, a helicopter offers troops on the ground many advantages over a fixed-wing aircraft. It is highly maneuverable and can fly lower, using mountains, trees, and buildings for cover. It can land in small areas to drop off soldiers, supplies, and ammunition or to pick up injured combatants and quickly carry them away.

The Korean War showed the need to arm helicopters in combat zones, and not long afterward, army tacticians began experimenting with the idea of an air cavalry. In the past, the cavalry had meant soldiers on horseback. During World War II, the name was given to armored tank units. In today's army it refers to soldiers who fight on vehicles, including airborne ones.

In Vietnam, the air cavalry would prove its value in a new kind of war fighting smaller enemy forces who would slip in and out of difficult terrain, and the helicopter became an important weapon in the U.S. arsenal. "Choppers" were a frequent sight in the skies above Vietnam. The first were armed with machine guns, primarily to provide protection when carrying troops, but as the war escalated, the military modified its utilitarian Huey helicopters into gunships equipped with machine guns and rocket launchers to escort the transports and

Choppers in Vietnam

fire on enemy forces. In 1968, the Cobra, the first dedicated attack helicopter, further expanded the air cavalry's role. With its increased speed and agility and better
protection for its crew, the Cobra could loiter in a con-
tested area and fire on enemy infantry and targets as
needed.

As modern weaponry developed, it became clear that
helicopters could deliver far more firepower than had
been previously thought. With their maneuverability, they
could keep delivering fire in a battle for a much longer
period than a fixed-wing plane could. More powerful

Two AH-64 Apache attack helicopters

machine guns, missiles, and more sophisticated navigation systems made the helicopter vital to modern warfare.

It was when the Apache attack helicopter was first introduced in the 1970s that close-combat aviation and close air support took giant leaps forward. The Apache was first placed into service in the 1980s and is now the U.S. Army's primary assault helicopter. It has an incredibly sophisticated weapons platform. Its computer software will connect with other Apaches', allowing multiple targets to be destroyed at once. The pilot's and co-pilot's helmets can be wired to control the machine gun mounted beneath the aircraft. The gun is aimed by simply turning the head and looking at the target.

Apache helicopters became an army staple in Iraq and Afghanistan. In a battle like Wanat, they could turn the tide. Usually insurgents and anti-Afghan forces would retreat when Apaches arrived on the scene.

Usually.

But not always.

THE CAVALRY ARRIVES

A CONFUSED PLATOON SERGEANT DAVID DZWIK WAITED

down in the command post. Radio communication with OP Topside had been abruptly cut off. He had no idea if the men had been killed or incapacitated or if the radio had been damaged. Trying to direct a defense of Topside with no information was not working. He decided to send more reinforcements.

Sergeant Dzwik pulled together nine men, including the platoon's acting medic and two of the marines who were embedded with the Afghan National Army. They brought along their M240 machine gun. Specialist Reid Grapes at the traffic-control point could see the enemy positions and guided Dzwik and his force through the gauntlet of enemy fire. He popped a smoke grenade to obscure the men as they climbed the terraces.

Just as Dzwik and his men made their mad dash toward OP Topside, two Apache attack helicopters appeared in the sky.

The arrival of the Apaches gave Second Platoon hope. The lead Apache, call sign Hedgerow 50, streaked down the valley toward OP Topside. Using the Apache's thermal sights, the gunner called out, "There is a guy right on the other side of the trees." The Apache fired its massive 30-mm cannon. The bullets rocketed into the earth mere meters from Topside's sandbags.

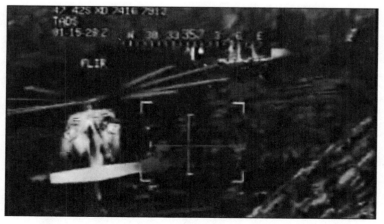

Hedgerow 50 or 53's view through its thermal camera on a gun run over Wanat. A medevac chopper is to the left; the burning missile truck at VPB Kahler is the white area at top center.

The second Apache, Hedgerow 53, swooped in. Paratroopers threw a green smoke grenade into the wash and dead brush to the east of Topside, where much of the enemy fire was coming from. Hedgerow 53 unloaded about fifty explosive rounds on the target. The helicopters pulled up and banked, ready for another gun run.

The conditions on the ground were so chaotic and the enemy so close to the American "friendlies" at OP Topside that the pilots had to be extremely precise.

It had been almost an hour since Myer first requested the air support.

Much like Chosen Company, the air squadron based in the area was required to provide close air support for a large area with limited resources. The two Apaches from Seventeenth Cavalry were based in Jalalabad, a thirty-minute flight away. The alert from Wanat came in at 4:30 a.m., but the Apaches needed time for their engines to warm up, and they didn't leave until 4:53 a.m. With the valley so confined, the helicopters had to pause at Blessing until the artillery stopped firing before it was safe to continue to Wanat.

Normally, the arrival of air support would cause the insurgents to disengage and retreat. That was not the case at Wanat. Despite the appearance of the Apaches,

GUN RUNS

When a forward observer calls in an air strike, the pilots will strafe the ground over a distance and toward the enemy with their machine guns. Pilots are able to place their fire with extreme accuracy to keep opposing forces at bay. Machine guns on current combat aircraft are capable of delivering thousands of rounds in a minute. Such overwhelming force usually causes enemy troops to quickly retreat.

the enemy fighters pulled back, but they did not retreat completely. Small-arms fire and rocket-propelled grenades continued to fall on OP Topside and VPB Kahler. The only solace was that because it was coming from farther away, the fire was much less accurate.

It was still causing injuries, though. Sergeant Dzwik and Specialist Aaron Davis, who had come up with him, were injured by shrapnel. With the Apaches continuing their gun runs, the insurgents shot grenades into the trees above Topside. The limbs and branches exploded, sending additional shrapnel and projectiles down on the soldiers below.

Shortly after the Apaches arrived, Captain Myer

made his way to OP Topside. Communications were not working properly. He needed a firsthand look at the situation and to observe the condition of his men. His main concern at this point was driving back the enemy and getting medevac helicopters in to carry away the wounded.

The medevac choppers would be sitting ducks. They would need to fly in and either land to pick up the wounded, or hover over the observation post and lift men one at a time by hoist. Neither choice was good.

The clock ticked on and the fight continued. Wounded and bleeding, Ryan Pitts was growing weaker by the minute. He remembered the guys starting "to come up to the OP from the Vehicle Patrol Base. I was seeing Sergeant Phillips. I think I saw Sergeant Dzwik. I was feeling relieved to see these guys. These are guys I've known for a long time and trust."

In spite of his grave injuries, he was working with the Apache gunners, relaying firing instructions by radio.

"I don't remember exactly when the Apaches came on station," he recalled later. "We trusted those guys. Over both deployments, I always had complete trust in the pilots that we had. I know they shot to the east of the OP, [and] to the northeast of the OP. They may have shot to the north. I wanted them to shoot five to ten meters to the north. I wanted them to come in west to east, so if they went long—they overshot—it would go away from the patrol base and the OP, and not toward it. And that was also the way the dead space ran, west to east, so I wanted them to fire in there to clear that out."

10
SUPPORT FROM FOB BLESSING

FOB Blessing
Kunar Province, Afghanistan
July 13, 2008, 4:30 a.m.

THE ALERT FOR IMMEDIATE MOVEMENT TO WANAT CAME

at half past four in the morning. Chosen Company's First Platoon jumped into action, loading four Humvees with reinforcements and extra ammunition.

First Platoon was the company's designated quick-reaction force, the unit selected to bring more firepower to any skirmish in the area. It was stationed at Forward Operating Base Blessing, five miles away. First Platoon was led by Lieutenant Aaron Thurman and Platoon Sergeant William Stockard. Sergeant Scott Beeson, the senior noncommissioned officer in Chosen Company, was going as well.

Armed and armored Humvees on the move

Two of their Humvees were equipped with grenade launchers. The other two had machine guns, a heavy-duty .50-caliber on one and an M240 on the other. It took a while to load the additional ammunition, but the Humvees didn't require night-operation devices. "The sun was starting to come up, so it wasn't too dark," Stockard later remembered. "We could see fine."

First Platoon was on the road by 5:15 a.m.

The road to Wanat from FOB Blessing held danger around every curve. Because it snaked through the mountain valley, there were multiple locations along the route that were ideal ambush spots. The road had not been cleared of improvised explosive devices, either.

No matter. With their fellow paratroopers in trouble, First Platoon did not approach with caution. Machine gunners shot into the underbrush and trees along the road. This "reconnaissance by fire" would expose any potential ambush that might prevent or delay the quick-reaction force. They arrived at VPB Kahler at approximately 6:00 a.m., making it in half the normal time.

While First Platoon was on its way, the Apaches continued their gun runs, driving the insurgents farther back. But when First Platoon rolled up, a strange thing happened. It appeared to rally the enemy forces. The gunfire and rocket-propelled grenades picked up. They were raining down on the area like lightning bolts. Several fires were burning, including the shell of the missile truck, dark smoke roiling from its metal skeleton and clouding the air. It caused poor visibility, preventing First Platoon from making a quick assessment of where their fellow paratroopers were located.

Sergeant Hissong at the traffic-control point tried to describe the situation for First Platoon. "When they arrived, I ran from my position to link up with them," Hissong recalled. "The first person I saw was Staff

Sergeant Silvernale. I don't remember the conversation, but he later told me that when I got to him, he asked me where the enemies were. He said I just looked around and didn't really answer him so he asked me again, and I said, 'I didn't know.' He said 'What do you mean you don't know?' And my response was '. . . They're everywhere, man.'"

Indeed, Hissong's report seemed accurate. Shots were coming from everywhere. There would be a temporary lull, then without warning it would swell again. The men of First Platoon knew their jobs. Their friends at VPB Kahler had been fighting for their lives for over an hour. It was up to them to help finish the battle by taking the fight to the enemy. After checking in with the command post, Sergeant Beeson, a radio man, and a medic immediately ran up to OP Topside.

Lieutenant Thurman was in his first combat action, but he organized his men immediately. He divided them into two squads. One followed Beeson up to Topside. It was easier now that the Apaches had driven the insurgents back. Thurman led the other squad in clearing the village of insurgents with two of the Humvees. While putting down heavy fire, they advanced on the enemy positions in the hotel and mosque. Their show of force sent the enemy into retreat. Lieutenant Thurman was employing the infantry tactic of "fire superiority." In modern warfare, it simply means returning fire with overwhelming force. This causes enemy fighters to pause, duck, hide, or withdraw, and disrupts their ability to shoot back. With automatic weapons, a single squad of four to eight infantrymen can return a ferocious volume of bullets. In many cases, this allows smaller units to drive back and even defeat a numerically superior enemy force.

When the attack started at 4:23 a.m., the men of Second Platoon had been greatly outnumbered and unable to establish fire superiority. Now the insurgents faced not only the Apaches' deadly runs, but also additional heavily armed paratroopers laying down withering fire from the Humvees. Though the insurgents were thrown back on their heels, they continued to pound VPB Kahler from all directions. The rocket-propelled grenades were particularly numerous.

The enemy attack would threaten the medevacs that were just now arriving at the site. The wounded were running out of time and needed evacuation. The mosque, hotel, and bazaar in the center of Wanat would have to be cleared. It would be a dangerous task. Thurman pressed the fight, ordering a dismounted attack.

Sergeant Kyle Silvernale took his squad to clear the hotel. Another volley of grenades erupted, injuring the sergeant. Nonetheless, Silvernale led his men on.

He recalled the operation in his report: "Moving to the northern end of the bazaar behind the second truck, I noticed a fresh blood trail leading through an overhang between the hotel and the building just north of the hotel. Pushing past the building just north of the hotel, my element came into heavy enemy contact once again. We started taking effective direct small arms fire from the north and east. Multiple enemy positions [were] to the east of our position, one directly behind the hotel . . . I moved into the bazaar and started clearance operations throughout the bazaar. Starting at the second-floor northeast corner of the hotel, clearing a foothold, I moved through the northeasternmost room to the window to throw [fragmentary grenades] down on the enemy position in a flanking maneuver."

Slowly, inch by hard-fought inch, the tide was turning. The wounded men of Second Platoon were ever closer to evacuation for the medical attention they desperately needed.

Sergeant Ryan Pitts up at OP Topside saw the medevac choppers fly into the valley. Despite reinforcements, the insurgents were putting up a stiff fight.

Pitts was weak and suffering from blood loss.

He needed a miracle.

DUSTOFF

THE TWO BLACK HAWK MEDEVAC CHOPPERS HAD BEEN

waiting at FOB Blessing. This would be a difficult operation. There was very little airspace in the steep-sided valley for aircraft to maneuver. That airspace was already being used by the two Apaches. Not to mention the fact that the enemy was shooting grenades and bullets all over the place, especially from the high ground around VPB Kahler.

There is perhaps no more vulnerable aircraft in a battle than a medevac chopper. The helicopter is equipped with guns for self-defense, but shooting back is not a priority. A medevac chopper can pick up soldiers in two ways: land on the ground or hover over a landing zone and slowly hoist the wounded up in a metal basket. Either way, the helicopter will almost certainly be exposed to enemy fire.

When Captain Myer reached OP Topside, he immediately called for the medevacs to come in. Dustoff 35 and Dustoff 36 zoomed into the valley. What they saw was chaos. The crews could hear machine-gun fire through the radio. As they drew closer, they could see insurgents moving from position to position on the ground. The landing zone at the command post was taking heavy fire from the enemy.

U.S. Army crewman strapped into the medevac hoist of a Black Hawk helicopter

Because the airspace was so crowded, only one med-evac could operate at a time. The flight plan called for Dustoff 35 to land first in a zone south of VPB Kahler and pick up the wounded down there. There was only one problem with this plan.

The smoke and dust from the fires and explosions reduced visibility, making landing dangerous. Para-troopers on the ground threw a violet smoke grenade to mark the zone, but Dustoff 35 had to make two passes over the battlefield before it could land safely. The aircraft received heavy fire. One crewman reported seeing an insurgent as close as ten feet from the con-certina wire that encircled the base. Dustoff 35 loaded five wounded soldiers and took off. It would take the wounded to the nearest field hospital.

Now it was Dustoff 36's turn. The plan called for a hoist maneuver over OP Topside. The Topside para-troopers threw another colored smoke grenade to mark the position, but the pilots could not identify it. They flew to the east and made another approach. On this turn, they spotted the violet smoke and de-cided to land on a nearby terrace that was just wide and flat enough to touch down. Their skill amazed everyone.

Ryan Pitts couldn't believe it. "A medevac bird came in and landed between where the OP was and one of the enemy fighting positions—one of their positions they engaged us pretty heavily from. When they threw smoke, I didn't believe that the helicopter was going to land there. It just seemed unfathomable. But they did, and it was probably one of the most incredible things I've ever seen."

Dustoff 36 had not only landed in a small, compact area, avoiding a slow and dangerous hoisting maneuver; it had landed *between* the men at OP Topside and the enemy, which was spraying the area with gunfire. The pilot of Dustoff 36 recalled, "There was yelling and screaming coming from the back of the aircraft. I could smell the gunpowder . . . from rounds expended in the firefight."

It was an amazing feat of skill and courage under fire—one to match that of Sergeant Ryan Pitts.

Sergeant Pitts had fought for over an hour, despite being critically wounded and briefly alone and running out of ammunition. He stayed at his post, helping to coordinate direct and indirect fire on the enemy. He had survived one of the bloodiest combat actions in the

Afghan war. Finally, he would be evacuated and get treatment for his wounds.

There were several times during the battle when Pitts could have been overtaken by the enemy. But he credits his fellow paratroopers and teammates for not letting that happen. "I think the other guys in the platoon made the enemy think twice about attempting to take the OP. They might have been able to overrun it, but they would have had to pay a dear price to take it."

THE AFTERMATH

THANKS TO DUSTOFF 35 AND DUSTOFF 36, RYAN PITTS
and his wounded platoon mates were safely on their way
to receive the medical treatment they desperately
needed. Pitts would later write to the medevac crew
chief, praising the pilots' daring actions.

At VPB Kahler the fight continued. More reinforcements arrived, from different units of the 503rd Rock
Regiment. Able Company's Third Platoon rolled up in
six Humvees at 8:20 a.m. Chinook helicopters ferried in
Battle Company's Third Platoon around 1:30 p.m. Eventually, U.S. and Afghan forces numbered more than two
hundred men on the ground.

Reconnaissance drone

Despite the reinforcements, the insurgents continued sporadic attacks through the evening and into the next day. They were engaged with artillery and mortar fire. Close air support came from fighter planes and helicopter gunships, and a drone was diverted to fly over the valley to provide aerial reconnaissance.

At first light on July 14, Wanat was searched building by building. As paratroopers moved through the village, they discovered massive amounts of spent shell casings and other areas where weapons had been stored. It soon became clear that insurgents had thoroughly infiltrated Wanat. Given the evidence left behind, it appeared they had had weeks to move weapons and fighters into the area. One small house had literally hundreds of shell casings from AK-47s, the machine gun favored by anti-coalition forces.

The insurgents had removed most of their dead and injured after the battle. This made it difficult to determine enemy casualties. Military intelligence analysts speculated that between twenty-five and fifty enemy fighters were killed.

Nine American soldiers died in the attack, and twenty-seven were wounded, including sixteen who needed immediate evacuation. Four Afghan National Army soldiers were wounded. Not counting helicopter crashes, the Battle of Wanat was the deadliest engagement in the Afghan war up to that point.

On July 15, orders came to withdraw all forces from Wanat. Trucks and helicopters arrived to remove men and equipment. After a review of the conflict, U.S. commanders had determined that there were not enough resources to properly support the patrol base.

The terrain was harsh and difficult to defend. The local civilian population was not willing to submit to the Afghan central government, and counterinsurgency methods had failed. The local police chief was arrested on suspicion of collaborating with the anti-Afghan

FALLEN COMRADES

*First Lieutenant
Jonathan P. Brostrom,
24, of Aiea, Hawaii*

*Sergeant Israel
Garcia, 24, of Long
Beach, California*

*Corporal Jonathan
R. Ayers, 24, of
Snellville, Georgia*

*Corporal Jason M.
Bogar, 25, of Seattle,
Washington*

*Corporal Jason
D. Hovater, 24, of
Clinton, Tennessee*

*Corporal Matthew
B. Phillips, 27, of
Jasper, Georgia*

*Corporal Pruitt A.
Rainey, 22, of Haw
River, North Carolina*

*Corporal Gunnar W.
Zwilling, 20, of
Florissant, Missouri*

*Specialist Sergio
S. Abad, 21, of
Morganfield, Kentucky*

insurgents. The civilian governor was also arrested, but later released.

Sergeant Ryan Pitts was eventually sent to Walter Reed National Military Medical Center in Washington, D.C., to recover from his wounds. At the hospital, he met Sergeant Israel Garcia's wife and mother. Garcia had asked Pitts in his last moments to tell them that he loved them. As he had promised, Pitts delivered Sergeant Garcia's final words to his loved ones.

Sergeant Pitts was originally nominated for a Distinguished Service Cross for his actions at the Battle of Wanat. But as the battle and Pitts's actions were more closely examined, a decision was made to upgrade the nomination to the Medal of Honor.

When he first heard about the nomination, Pitts was not happy. He didn't think he deserved the recognition. He and his fellow soldiers had fought as a team. They'd fought for each other. He felt he owed his life to the men in his platoon, especially the nine fallen heroes.

"I wouldn't be here today if it weren't for them . . . The award belongs to them and every man who fought at Vehicle Patrol Base Kahler."

Later, Ryan Pitts came to look at the award as a testament to his friends. "I know I've been given a gift, and

I have an appreciation of life that I didn't have before. I know now that I am going to live my life to the fullest and enjoy it for those who aren't here. I owe it to them."

Sergeant Pitts was awarded the Medal of Honor at the White House on July 21, 2014. The ceremony was especially poignant because it included family members of the nine men of Chosen Company who died at Wanat. After President Barack Obama called out the name of each fallen soldier, he asked the families to stand and be recognized. On that day, Sergeant Pitts became only the ninth living person to receive the Medal of Honor for service in Afghanistan or Iraq.

As President Obama noted, "In Ryan Pitts, you see the humility and the loyalty that define America's men and women in uniform. Of this medal, Pitts says, 'It's not mine alone. It belongs to everybody who was there that day, because we did it together.'"

Sergeant Pitts retired from the army in 2009. Despite his wounds and the loss of his brothers-in-arms, he says of his time in the military: "It was the greatest thing I've ever done in my life. And it was the honor of my lifetime to serve with those guys. I would do it all over again."

On July 13, 2008, Sergeant Ryan Pitts earned his place among the Medal of Honor fraternity. His actions

Sergeant Ryan Pitts receiving the Medal of Honor from President Barack Obama, July 21, 2014

that day set an example for everyone in how to overcome fear and persevere, even against sometimes overwhelming odds. Still, like most who are awarded a Medal of Honor, he does not consider himself a hero.

"The word *hero* gets thrown out with the award, and I hate that word. For me, it's always been reserved for those that make the ultimate sacrifice. Those guys are the real heroes. And those guys that day were Sergio

Abad, Jonathan Ayers, Jason Bogar, Jonathan Brostrom, Israel Garcia, Jason Hovater, Matthew Phillips, Pruitt Rainey, and Gunnar Zwilling. Those guys are my heroes. Along with many of the other guys that I served with."

Heroes indeed.

RYAN M. PITTS'S
MEDAL OF HONOR CITATION

THE PRESIDENT OF THE UNITED STATES OF AMERICA,
AUTHORIZED BY ACT OF CONGRESS, MARCH 3, 1863,
HAS AWARDED IN THE NAME OF CONGRESS
THE MEDAL OF HONOR
TO SERGEANT RYAN M. PITTS
UNITED STATES ARMY

FOR CONSPICUOUS GALLANTRY AND INTREPIDITY AT THE RISK
OF HIS LIFE ABOVE AND BEYOND THE CALL OF DUTY:

Sergeant Pitts distinguished himself by extraordinary acts of heroism at the risk of his life above and beyond the call of duty while serving as a forward observer in 2d Platoon, Chosen Company, 2d Battalion (Airborne), 503d Infantry Regiment, 173d Airborne Brigade, during combat operations against an armed enemy at Vehicle Patrol Base Kahler vicinity of Wanat village, Kunar Province, Afghanistan, on July 13, 2008. Early that morning, while Sergeant Pitts was providing perimeter security at Observation Post Topside, a well-organized Anti-Afghan Force consisting of over 200 members initiated a close proximity sustained and complex assault using accurate and intense rocket-propelled grenade, machine gun and small arms fire on Wanat Vehicle Patrol Base. An immediate wave of rocket-propelled grenade rounds engulfed the Observation Post, wounding Sergeant Pitts and inflicting heavy casualties. Sergeant Pitts had been knocked to the ground and was bleeding heavily from shrapnel wounds to his arm and legs, but with incredible toughness and resolve, he subsequently took control of the Observation Post and returned fire on the enemy. As the enemy drew nearer, Sergeant Pitts threw grenades, holding them after the pin was pulled and the safety lever was released to allow a nearly immediate detonation on the hostile forces. Unable to stand on his own and near death because of the severity of his wounds and blood loss, Sergeant Pitts continued to lay suppressive fire until a two-man reinforcement team arrived. Sergeant Pitts quickly assisted them by giving up his main weapon and gathering ammunition, all while continually lobbing fragmentary grenades until these were expended. At this point, Sergeant Pitts crawled to the northern position radio and described the situation to the Command Post as the enemy continued to try and isolate the Observation Post from the main Patrol Base. With the enemy close enough for him to hear their voices and with total disregard for his own life, Sergeant Pitts whispered in radio situation reports and conveyed information that the Command Post used to provide indirect fire support. Sergeant Pitts' courage, steadfast commitment to the defense of his unit and ability to fight while seriously wounded prevented the enemy from overrunning the observation post and capturing fallen American soldiers, and ultimately prevented the enemy from gaining fortified positions on higher ground from which to attack Wanat Vehicle Patrol Base. Sergeant Ryan M. Pitts' extraordinary heroism and selflessness above and beyond the call of duty are in keeping with the highest traditions of military service and reflect great credit upon himself, Company C, 2d Battalion (Airborne), 503d Infantry Regiment, 173d Airborne Brigade and the United States Army.

KEY TERMS

airborne Troops trained to enter combat after transport by air, either parachuting in or touching down. Soldiers must complete three weeks of airborne school at Fort Benning, Georgia, to become paratroopers.

AK-47 A Soviet-designed, gas-operated automatic rifle. Tough and inexpensive to manufacture, it is favored by the Taliban and other anti-Afghan insurgents.

Al Queda A terrorist group founded by Osama bin Laden. The name is Arabic for "the base."

ANA or **Afghan National Army** The military force of the Afghan central government. This army of Afghan nationals was first developed in 2002 by the United States, which still oversees its training today.

anti-Afghan forces Any forces fighting U.S. and coalition forces in Afghanistan. They include local militias and criminal cartels that are opposed to the central government and the U.S. presence in Afghanistan, as well as radical Islamic groups like the Taliban and Al Queda and their transnational supporters.

close air support Action by aircraft against enemy targets close to friendly forces that requires detailed coordination with forces on the ground. The aircraft provide indirect fire, and the person on the ground calling for the fire is responsible for its effect. Helicopters or specialized aircraft such as the A-10 Warthog are usually involved.

close-combat aviation Action similar to close air support, except the aircraft provide direct fire, and the air crew is responsible for the fire's effects. Attack helicopters such as Apaches are usually involved.

concertina wire Coiled barbed or razor wire that can be expanded like an accordion or concertina. Used as a perimeter defense, it entangles and jams the wheels or tracks of an oncoming vehicle.

dustoff A medical evacuation of wounded personnel by helicopter.

FOB or **forward operating base** Officially, an airfield that is used to support military operations. In practice, the home bases of the majority of U.S. soldiers in Afghanistan. They vary widely in size, from major air bases with thousands of soldiers to small outposts with little more than bunkers and tents and no plumbing. FOB Blessing was in the middle, with a dining hall, showers, and a weight room.

grenade A small explosive or chemical bomb thrown by hand or fired by a grenade launcher. M67 fragmentation grenades can spread shrapnel within a fifty-foot radius.

howitzer A cannon used to fire shells using relatively high trajectories and low velocities over long distances.

Humvee A high-mobility multipurpose wheeled vehicle, usually a four-wheel-drive, multipurpose truck designed to move troops around quickly. Humvees are armored and can have mounted weapons such as machine guns and missile or grenade launchers.

indirect fire Weapons aimed by coordinates or other measurements, where the operator does not have a direct line of sight to the target. Such weapons include artillery, rockets, and mortars.

medevac A helicopter used for emergency evacuation of the sick or wounded.

OP or **observation post** A position, sometimes elevated, from which a squad can observe an assigned area and its avenues of approach, and direct fire.

pulling security Standing watch, looking for any enemy movement. Also called guard duty.

quick-reaction force An uncommitted, highly mobile military unit designated to respond to emergency calls from other units operating in the area.

reconnaissance by fire Shooting into positions where there is a reasonable suspicion of enemy presence. Designed to expose and prevent any potential attack.

RPG or rocket-propelled grenade An explosive fired by a shoulder-mounted rocket launcher.

stand to To stand ready for an attack, especially before dawn or after dusk.

suppressing fire Rapid direct or indirect fire delivered in response to enemy fire, with the goal of preventing any more enemy fire.

Taliban A Sunni Islamic fundamentalist religious and political group based primarily in Afghanistan. The name comes from the Pashto word for "students."

VPB or vehicle patrol base A base to provide security and reconnaissance in an assigned area.

NOTES

6 "it definitely felt like": Ryan Pitts, "In His Own Words," in U.S. Army, "Medal of Honor."

9 "a little bit odd": Pitts, "In His Own Words," in U.S. Army, "Medal of Honor."

16 "On September the 11th": George W. Bush, "Address to a Joint Session of Congress," Sept. 20, 2001, teachingamericanhistory.org/library /document/address-to-a-joint-session-of-congress.

21 "I'd been a little shell-shocked": Pitts, interview by Herbert, Aug. 7, 2014.

23 "My line of thinking": Pitts, "In His Own Words," in U.S. Army, "Medal of Honor."

28 "My graduating class": This and the following three quotations are from Ryan Pitts, interview by Paul Herbert, Aug. 7, 2014.

31 "All these guys": This and the following quote are from Ryan Pitts, "'When the Guys Go, They Take a Part of You with Them': Surviving the Battle of Wanat," interview by David Siry, April 18, 2016, West Point Center for Oral History, video, 1:08:16, westpointcoh.org /interviews/when-the-guys-go-they-take-a-part-of-you-with -them-surviving-the-battle-of-wanat.

31 "That was kind of my first baptism": Pitts, interview by Herbert.

39 "Later on—I don't": Pitts, "In His Own Words," in U.S. Army, "Medal of Honor."

40 "Me and Ayers": U.S. Army Combat Studies Institute, p. 155.

42 "[I] got on the radio": Pitts, interview by Herbert.

42 "I thought it was my time": Pitts, "Reluctant Hero."

43 "I was putting them right": U.S. Army Combat Studies Institute, p. 160.

50 "extraordinary heroism": Presidential Unit Citation, 32 *Code of Federal Regulations* 578.57.

51 "Sergeant said in a hushed tone": U.S. Army Combat Studies Institute, p. 161.

53 "I definitely felt relief": Pitts, "In His Own Words," in U.S. Army, "Medal of Honor."

54 "That's when my position was hit": This and the next quotation by Denton are from U.S. Army Combat Studies Institute, p. 162.

55 "Denton started pulling": This and the next quotation by Pitts are from U.S. Army Combat Studies Institute, pp. 162–3.

63 "There is a guy": U.S. Army Combat Studies Institute, p. 163.

66 "to come up to the OP": Pitts, "In His Own Words," in U.S. Army, "Medal of Honor."

66 "I don't remember exactly when": Pitts, "In His Own Words," in U.S. Army, "Medal of Honor."

69 "The sun was starting": This and the following two quotations from Hissong and Silvernale in this chapter are from U.S. Army Combat Studies Institute, pp. 167–170.

78 "A medevac bird came in": Pitts, "In His Own Words," in U.S. Army, "Medal of Honor."

78 "There was yelling": U.S. Army Combat Studies Institute, p. 173.

79 "I think the other guys": Pitts, interview by Herbert.

84 "I wouldn't be here today": Pitts, "Reluctant Hero."

84 "I know I've been given": Pitts, "Reluctant Hero."

85 "In Ryan Pitts, you see": Barack Obama, "Remarks by the President at Presentation of the Medal of Honor to Staff Sergeant Ryan Pitts," July 21, 2014, Obama White House Archives, go.wh.gov /hfsRUU.

85 "It was the greatest thing": Ryan Pitts, press conference, Concord, N.H., June 26, 2014, transcript at army.mil/article/129289/ryan_pitts _medal_of_honor_press_conference.

86 "The word *hero*": Pitts, interview by Herbert.

SELECTED BIBLIOGRAPHY

Bernstein, Jonathan. *AH-64 Apache Units of Operations Enduring Freedom and Iraqi Freedom*. Oxford, U.K.: Osprey, 2005. This guidebook to the Apache helicopter details its use during combat, with a particular emphasis on its deployment in Iraq and Afghanistan.

Collier, Peter. *Medal of Honor: Portraits of Valor Beyond the Call of Duty*. Photo by Nick Del Calzo. 3rd ed. New York: Artisan, 2011. This book profiles 144 medal winners who fought in engagements from World War II to Iraq and Afghanistan. Heavily illustrated with photographs, the book also comes with a DVD.

Mraz, Steve. "Soldiers Recount Deadly Attack on Afghanistan Outpost." *Stars and Stripes*, July 19, 2008. stripes.com/news/soldiers-recount -deadly-attack-on-afghanistan-outpost-1.81141.

Pitts, Ryan. "Reluctant Hero Ryan Pitts." Interview by Greg Heilshorn. *New Hampshire Magazine*, August 2014. nhmagazine.com/August -2014/Reluctant-Hero-Ryan-Pitts.

———. Interview by Paul Herbert. Aug. 7, 2014. Pritzker Military Museum & Library. Video, 1:06. pritzkermilitary.org/whats_on/medal -honor/medal-honor-recipient-ryan-pitts. Sergeant Pitts discusses his deployments in Afghanistan and gives a thorough recounting of the Battle of Wanat.

Richardson, Doug, and Lindsay Peacock. *Combat Aircraft: AH-64 Apache*. London: Salamander Books, 1992.

U.S. Army. "Medal of Honor: Staff Sergeant Ryan Pitts; The Battle." army.mil/medalofhonor/pitts/battle/index.html. This website is an incredible resource for studying the Battle of Wanat. It offers recollections from the soldiers who participated as well as photographs, maps, and video reenactments of the events as they unfolded.

————. "Wanat Review." June 22, 2010. army.mil/article/41241/wanat
-review.

U.S. Army Combat Studies Institute. *Wanat: Combat Action in Afghanistan, 2008*. Fort Leavenworth, KS: Combat Studies Institute Press,
2010. armyupress.army.mil/Portals/7/combat-studies-institute/csi
-books/Wanat.pdf. This definitive account of the Battle of Wanat is
nearly three hundred pages and includes official after-action reports,
illustrations, and statements from Ryan Pitts and numerous other
soldiers of Chosen Company.

Willbanks, James H., ed. *America's Heroes: Medal of Honor Recipients from
the Civil War to Afghanistan*. Santa Barbara, CA: ABC-CLIO, 2011.
Written in an encyclopedic format, this book profiles two hundred
Medal of Honor winners. It includes photographs and a list of all
the recipients of the medal.

Zoroya, Gregg. *The Chosen Few: A Company of Paratroopers and Its Heroic
Struggle to Survive in the Mountains of Afghanistan*. Boston, MA:
DaCapo Press, 2017. This is an exhaustive history of Chosen Company's time in Afghanistan. The author is a journalist who was embedded with the company for a time. It covers both deployments and
ends with vivid descriptions of the Battle of Wanat.